Stars, Stripes and The Healer Within

...A Tribute to 9/11

Poetry by Tatiana Babic
Photography By Alvarez Wortham

Dedication

To all those who are healing their wounds and believing that every one of us is empowered to co-create a better world.

Acknolwledgements

I would like to thank all those helping Angels who either assisted me in the preperation of this book or provided me with emotional support and motivational inspiration. The following have my deepest gratitude:
Alvarez Wortham for sharing his extraordinary talant with the rest of us- Thank you Christina and Michael for going with me through thick and thin- also thanks to Ira Israel, Dan Greene, Jimmy Sacco, Roger Cook, Suzanne Fowler, Lisa Mandelbaum, Anthony Barnes, Sandra and Joe, Ben and Robin ,Aranka Israni , Lori and Dave and ,last but definitely not least ,thanks to Andrea Schneider for contributing her beautiful photographs to this project.

DreamScape Publishing
3734 Vinton Ave., Suite 1
Los Angeles, CA 90034

Stars, Stripes and The Healer Within.

ISBN 0-9722785-0-8

Printed in Hong Kong

Library of Congress Control Number: 2002109328

Published by DreamScape Publishing
Printer: Pacific Rim
Cover design: Aranka Israni—www.arankai.com
Contributed photographs by Andrea Schneider:
1. contemplate
2. prayer
3. believe
4. solidarity

Introduction

This book is dedicated to the resilience of the human spirit and the inevitable healing process that must take place in wake of the events of September 11, 2001. It is a process that requires our attention, for healing does not happen by accident. In order for our wounds to properly and permanently heal, the process must be active and deliberate.

This piece of art documents the binding forces in America after a day when the unimaginable became all-too real. When I look back on the deadly attacks, I try to comprehend the full horror experienced by the entire world. I observed how our paradigms fell and then rose again when tested by such a devastating catastrophe. Is there a hidden lesson in this experience that we must learn?

On September 11th, I was coming back from a European vacation on a plane from Berlin to Los Angeles via Paris. My plane was amongst the hundreds of planes grounded in the wake of the attacks. I spent some time in Paris before flying back to Berlin to wait there for a flight out. Finally, when I was able to fly back to Los Angeles, I brought home a memory of a valuable revelation: that all civilized people were united in mourning. Both Paris and Berlin seemed to have stopped breathing; they were paralyzed. Everything looked different–people, birds, dogs, cars, trees, stores. Everything! A dark cloud spread from every living creature over traffic to every single brick in every wall numbing all senses and interrupting the flow of our existence. The speed of life switched in an instant to slow motion. On the streets, on subways and on buses, people walked and sat with lowered heads and watery eyes. There were barely any sounds. The silence was painful. It seemed as if this prevailing grief was spreading like wildfire through almost every pore of civilization. The attacks were caused by a long history of conflicting interests, but the effects of the attacks reached beyond all known boundaries and struck at the core of the security of humanity.

On one hand there was grief and despair; on the other hand there were countless reunions, intense introspection and consummate changes in individuals' priorities. Friends and family members who held *longtime grudges reconciled and started talking again. People were struck by the sudden awareness of having given up the precious gift of a loved one for a banal bagatelle. People started reevaluating their lives and cherishing the present rather than being a slave to the uncertain future. How long this new virtue is going to be part of our reality is up to every person individually. We cannot erase from history or from our hearts the events of September 11th. Now we must decide how we are going to remember that infamous day and what are we going to learn from it. Let's not forget it is a choice; a choice that we make as individuals and as a collective consciousness.*

When I arrived back in Los Angeles, another awareness dawned on me: the American flag had become a symbol of something beyond patriotism. It was being used not only by Americans but by people around the globe to express empathy and compassion for the victims of the recent events. The red, white and blue flag rising up like a phoenix sent the message "I am part of this." Being a Croatian-born German, I never, not for one moment, felt separated from this shocking experience. And now more than ever, I realize that it is one world, one cause, one effect, and one people sitting together in a small rocky boat.

Just by parading the Star-Spangled Banner in all shapes and sizes, a contribution to the healing process was made. There were flags on people's clothing, on cars, in homes and businesses. They were all over the place, screaming and waving, reaching out to be heard, reaching out to be seen. They stood up proudly and wanted to be photographed and remembered. Alvarez, the photographer, was the eyes and I was the ears. Every call was different from the other. Some were controversial and provoking, some touched the heart, some were cute and funny and some were simply beautiful. These were outcries from the depth of our beings revealing how we feel and, more importantly, that we feel. Originally the poetry was not planned, but after experiencing an emotional roller coaster ride as I took in the photographs, poems started pouring out of me onto the paper and I became the voice for these flags.

I invite you to take in these few pages with an open mind and let inspiration carry you to the horizon of infinite possibilities. Be a witness to the kind of magic that creates a space for an expanded awareness, an expanded consciousness, for peace, and for love.

9/11

vicious cowardly unbearable unjustly horrific blank unreal

necessary?

senseless inexplicable heartbreaking terrified remember

anxious nauxious disconnected atrocious katastrophic

disillusioning insane surreal frozen sad emotional

brutal hideous nervous incomprehensible terrible dreadful

awful

horrendous appalling shock ghastly frightening painful distressing

rage fear nightmare

anger savagery barbarity fury insanity

madness

respond **why?** unbelievable panic

daze hell stupor alarm trepidation

reality tears

chaos screams dust sirens

heartrending lurid trapped

Torn

All you victims of anger,
Children of hatred and despise
Can't you smell the dope of sabotage in the back of your brain?

Mind games like Thousands of knives
Piercing your own self
And no one else

Pointing fingers
Being satisfied with a quick numbing of the emptiness
Just for a blink,
A blink it is

Black, white, yellow, green
Isn't it the same pain that we all feel?

Who is to blame?
Where is the shame?

Separated and yet one,
Dance with the wind of change
You have the power
Show me the will

I am starting to hum
Can you continue to sing?

"Curbs of L.A."

ANS
ARTS BLDG.
9200

United We Stand
Divided We Fall
Victory for All Americans!
FEEL THE SPIRIT OF MARTHA RAYE HELP PROTECT THE USA

“Tears”

“Pride”

AUTOMOTIVE
DATSUN
California
6M97117

“Journey“

Hope

Where to be found?
Endless search in the streets of mind
The haunting grays of dusty alleys leading towards
Nowhere

One dead end after another
Despair at every corner
Constant struggle of doubts
And fear

If there wasn't that
Fire
Roaring flames whispering deep inside
You know, You know

I know

She does not live in the mind
Her home is the heart

That hope

“In The Middle Of Nowhere”

Time, a healer?

Time does not heal
never has
never will

Time

What a great magician?
The illusion of movement,
of passing, of winning, of losing
Dripping
into the dungeon
down my throat

Illusion

Tricking me into staying captured,
held as a hostage
Blindfolded

For a moment I am still
looking up at the imprisoning walls
reaching out for the cold, dark guards
and seeing them
Dissolve

I
Did
It !

Time does not heal
never has

Garden State
WORLD PEACE
WE
ARE NOT AFRAID

“Remember“

Septemb
11
2001

The Lesson

I was bowing deep to her
feet
Entered this plane like a planted
seed
My roots firmly bonded with her
soil
She deserves better than this
turmoil
Earth, my mother, heart of
red
Alive and yet so
sad

Tears of Gaia dropping into the deep blue
mystery
Widening the waters of
ocean
Haven't they learned from this planet's
history?
Humans, constantly settling for a destructive
notion

Is this another one of those passing-by lessons?
Untouched by responsibility
        Hidden from integrity
                Missed out on humanity
                        Abused frailty
What will YOU take home from this insanity?

Earth's salty wet playing on my
tongue
Giving away her secret like a majestic
song
Such a splendid light of wisdom and
grace
Illuminating my little body, my infinite soul
Through my hands, the waters of her
face

WESTWOOD MEDICAL
LIBERTY AND
JUSTICE
9-11

UNITE

Come closer
You relief of mine
Free me from the deep cutting pain
Lingering in my heart,
In my throat, in my soul of time

Come closer
Free me from uncertainty,
Racing through my veins,
Poisoning my flesh and my dreams

Come closer
You hero of mine
With no solution, only calming warmth
Our souls deeply intertwine

Come closer
Tighter, squeeze me so I can't breathe
Carrying the cross along with me,
Bleeding together in unity

Come closer
My love
Lift the unbearable weight of my back
Of my mind
Hold the flag
And unite

BRAGA RANCH'S
FREEDOM FENCE
BY LOCAL SCHOOLS
PLEASE DONATE TO THE RED CROSS

Gonzales 8
Salinas 24
San Francisco 130

GABILAN SCHOOL
Ms Bravo Kinder Class
United We Stand

Before
After
With Liberty and Justice 4 All!

United We Stand

“Contemplate“

“Prayer“

“Believe“

“Solidarity“

NO PARKING
24 HOUR
ACTIVE DRIVEWAY
CAB WATCH
NEW YORK
8B90A
TAXI

F.D.
N.Y.
DEDICATED IN MEMORY OF THE MEMBERS OF LADDER 11
WHO MADE THE SUPREME SACRIFICE
LT. MICHAEL QUILTY
FF. EDWARD DAY
FF. JOHN HEFFERNAN
9-11-01
FF. RICHARD KELLY
FF. MATTHEW ROGAN
FF. MICHAEL CAMMARATA
We Will Never Forget
DANGER
11

FDNY
LADDER

F.D.N.Y.
LAVAN

“Salute Our Heroes“

NYC
& COMPANY
SALUTE OUR
HEROES
WWW.TWINTOWERSFUND.COM
CANTOR
Fitzgerald

“Empathy“

"*Walk Of Memories*"

FROM AROUND TH WORLD
THEIR PRAYERS AND SUPPORT

ground zero 1

look at me
what have i become?
a pile of weeping dust
a heap of stinking dirt

the hot sticky summer air
lays its head
on my cushion of
sweet sour debris
suppressing my memories of
strength and invulnerability
penetrating my dream of
safety ...

THANK YOU
We Will Never
Forget Them
We Will Never
Forget You
WE NY

Ground Zero 2

Like The Phoenix From The Ashes
I Will Rise
Stand Taller Than Ever
To Mesmerize
Leave Behind The Doomed Screams,
The Shattered Dreams

Worship In Every Reborn Brick Of Mine
Remembrance Of Soul
A Temple
A Shrine

Like A Pagoda
On Western Ground
I Will Keep The Treasures
Of Sacred Sound

I Will Fuse Every Tear
With Every Drop Of Sweat
In Ceremony
To Build The Anchor Of My Foundation,
My Heart
On This Battered Field
Of Memory

WTC
LAW ENFORCEMENT
RESCUE/RECOVERY TEAM
POLICE

“reflect“

QM1A
QM11
QM24

Awakening

Was it just a quiet feather's cry
That made me open my eye
So subtle and sweet,
That woke me, from a life long sleep?

A cry

For wings need to be free
They were born to see

Stretching out the rusty thoughts to the heavens
Bending and twisting in circles and spirals
For understanding of the lessons

Transforming from cocoon to butterfly
I sink on my knees
And start to cry
Recognizing the beauty of living, of life

Taking the very first breath, so fresh
Dreaming,
Drifting,
Gazing through a phlegmatic blink of an eyelash

Or was it the sound of wind
Blowing through the wings of a dragonfly
The reflection of the sun
Tickling her colors
That invited me to the home of questions,
Like...why?
Bowing to the breeze,
Brushing away the dust of dried tears
And sorrows

Gracefully allowing tears of happiness and bliss,
Awakening to life's kiss
A moment of
Awareness
From darkness to light
Will hopefully
Silence
The enduring fight

“Freedom“

"We are not mad, we are human, we want to love, and someone must forgive us for the paths we take to love, for the paths are many and dark, and we are ardent and cruel in our journey."

– Leonard Cohen